Style Made Simple
Non-Fiction

Text copyright © 2019 by Erin Busbee

Any names, characters, places, events, incidents, similarities or resemblance to actual persons, living or dead, events, or places, is entirely coincidental. All rights reserved. Except as permitted under the US Copyright Act of 1976, no part of this publication may be reproduced, stored in a retrieval system, or transmitted in any form or by any means electronic, mechanical, photocopying, recording, or otherwise, without written permission of the author. For information regarding permission, send a query to the author. Every effort has been made to ensure that the content provided herein is accurate, up-to-date, and helpful to the reader at the time of this publishing. This document contains affiliate links for which the author will receive a commission if purchases are made. The author does not guarantee any results, experience, or product based on any affiliate link. Visit www.busbeestyle.com for more information about the author, updates, or new books.

INTRO
My Story — 04

PART ONE
Getting Started — 11
Style Challenges | Body Shapes | Measurements
Well-Fitted Bra | Long vs Short-Waisted | Style Type

PART TWO
Getting Detailed — 33
Wardrobe Basics Part 1 | Wardrobe Basics Part 2
Dressing Your Age | Key Styling Tips | Fashion Fix Its

PART THREE
Getting Organized — 66
Closet Editing | Closet Organization

PART FOUR
Shopping — 74
Shopping | Now You're Ready

EXTRAS
Terminology & FAQs — 82

> **Having a limited budget was my first true fashion challenge.**

my STORY

Believe it or not, there have been many times when I struggled with my style. In fact, when I first moved to New York City, I stuck out like a country bumpkin. I'll share more about that experience in a moment.

Being one of four children with a single mom and no financial support from dad meant my mom sewed our clothes to save money. As I got older, second-hand stores and outlets became a lifeline, helping me find stylish and affordable pieces. My first professional job also helped me find my way. Having a limited budget was my first true fashion challenge, and it taught me to be creative with what I had. To this day, one of my superpowers is being able to walk into an outlet or thrift store and find the style treasures!

When I graduated from college, I fought for a job as a news reporter and quickly discovered the joys of working overnight shifts in order to prepare for the early morning news show. Buying suits and other professional outfits on a $16,000 a year salary is VERY tough! I pretty much lived at T.J. Maxx!

Working those hours also meant no social life. At the time, friends were scarce. Money was so short I had to waitress on the side, and living at home with my mom was the only option. My hustling life wasn't exactly

At **Machu Picchu** in Peru.

what I'd envisioned.

Then I experienced a loss that changed my entire world: My dad died at fifty-one years old. On the day he died, without knowing something was wrong, I called in sick to work. Because of an intuitive feeling, I jumped in my car and started driving home without telling anyone my plan. At this point in my career, I was working in Rochester, NY a few hours away from my hometown. When I was just a half-hour away, I called my brother-in-law and asked, "I'm on my way there. Should I come to your house or dad's house?"

He answered quietly and quickly. "Your dad's house." I knew in that moment my dad was gone. I calmly asked, "He's gone, isn't he?"

"Yes," he replied gently. "He died minutes ago."

My sister sensed it, too. She called in sick to work that day as well, as if she also knew. Neither of us discussed this until much later. Isn't it amazing how intuition works?

Although my relationship with my dad was strained and painful, feelings of loss and sadness completely overwhelmed me. Once I arrived at my dad's house, I got out of my car and my knees literally buckled underneath me. I collapsed into the soft, cold grass, crying uncontrollably. My dad would never be the dad I had hoped and prayed for. He would never enjoy the life I imagined he could have had. A life full of light, joy, and love.

This experience taught me many things, including the fragility

ERIN BUSBEE | STYLE MADE SIMPLE

Our Wedding in West Texas.

> "Life was simply too short to live a life I did not love."

and preciousness of life. After we buried my dad, I went back to Rochester a new person. Life was simply too short to live a life I did not love. I wasn't going to work one more overnight shift. Within days, I devised a plan to move to New York City (something I had always dreamed of doing). I quit my job, packed up, and headed to New York City. Even though I didn't have a job lined up, I felt confident. Within a couple of months, I landed my first job as an executive assistant to the president for the Miss Universe Organization.

Have you ever seen **The Devil Wears Prada?** My boss was like a younger version of Miranda Priestly. Her coffee had to be the exact right temperature, or she demanded another. She barked orders to everyone and terrified most of the office with her prickly demeanor and incessant, diva-like demands. There was no room for error.

One day she called me into her office and commanded, "Go to Bergdorf and get a baby gift." The gift was for a former Miss Universe.

I was always happy for an excuse to get out of the toxic office, but the weight of the task caught me off guard. After standing outside the beautiful Bergdorf Goodman facade for about ten minutes, I finally worked up the courage to walk in. I will never forget how frightened I felt in that moment. I quickly I scanned the store, hoping to find a gift before some snobby salesperson asked, "Can I help you?" and scanned me

Eight months **pregnant with Elizabeth.**

with her cold, knowing eyes. No doubt she would immediately size up my inexpensive clothing and wonder, **why is she here?**

That's when I realized I had work to do. I really had *no clue* about the world I had entered in New York City. I didn't know anything about fashion. I knew nothing about designers, department stores, or labels. In this world, I stood out in a bad way, like a country bumpkin or the country mouse in the city. My Gap chinos weren't cutting it here! No one was going to take me seriously, so I needed to buckle down and learn, because I desperately wanted to feel like *I did* belong in that store and all the others like it dotting 5th Avenue.

I immediately started studying designers, trends, and streetstyle with the voraciousness of an eager student. My gaze tracked other women in the street to see what they were wearing. I dove into magazines, style books, anything I could get my hands on. (This was before the Internet and *What Not To Wear.*) Learning what I needed to learn so I could look the part and walk into *those stores* with confidence, knowing that *I did* belong there, was my main focus.

And I did it!

With time, study, persistence, and dedication, I found my passion in fashion. With my newfound confidence and knowledge, I landed back into TV news and found my dream job as the Entertainment Producer at WCBS. (The job was such a luxury that it no longer exists now!) Now, not only would I walk into *those* stores like Bergdorf without hesitation, but my co-workers

ERIN BUSBEE | STYLE MADE SIMPLE

regularly asked me for style advice. I shopped and styled many news reporters and anchors, which planted the seed for my wardrobe styling business later on.

I had finally arrived! My style work was done. Or so I thought.

When I was thirty-one years old, I met my husband, Chris. The six-foot-two, Texan, former football player, world-traveler, banker. (That sounds like a line from a Coolio song!) After we dated for several months, he mailed me a gift card to my favorite steak restaurant in New York City for my birthday. I realized that he not only remembered my birthday, but he also remembered my favorite restaurant! It was that small, but telling gesture that made me realize, he is **the one.**

I called him immediately, thanked him, and invited him to dinner—using my gift card, of course. We married about two years later. We settled into our happy married life, and eventually the next step that would challenge me more than I ever dreamed.

We had children.

If New York City challenged my style, it was nothing compared to what my kids did to me. There's no way to truly prepare for your post-baby body, because you never know what it will be. It's different for everyone.

Thanks to pregnancy with my

Our family moved to Telluride Colorado - Halloween 2017.

son, Gage, I gained fifty pounds. I would love to sit here and tell you that after having Gage, I was reveling in the miracle of life and how glorious my body is. But, the truth is, I was pretty traumatized by what I saw. This new body wasn't mine! Trying to dress this version of myself was a whole new style challenge I was not prepared for. I felt like a mess.

Just like with other style challenges, I worked through that one too—with some studying, patience, and lots of grace.

My most recent style challenge is something we all face: aging. Even though I still feel like I'm thirty, I just turned forty-five, and I have made modifications to my style. I used to wear shorter skirts and dresses, but now I really think twice before I put on a short skirt or dress. Modifying can feel scary or limiting! Not only that, but it can cause an overwhelming sense of uncertainty while shopping. This paralyzing feeling happens even to me, who has literally made a career out of shopping and styling women! I really want to look modern and current, but my new fears are always in the back of my mind. **Do I look like I'm trying too hard?** It's a fine line. None of us want to slowly descend into frump town, become invisible, or worse still … look desperate to reclaim youth.

That's why I created this guide for you.

On many levels, I know what it feels like to struggle with style. I know from experience! I have lived through the **very real** struggles, whether it's not knowing enough, or feeling overwhelmed by too many choices. Whether it's budget, lack of confidence, fear, transitioning to a new phase of life, motherhood, or all of these, I've been through it. I am still going through it! There are ways to figure out what works for you right now, how to dress the body you have right **now**, and how to make style simple. Yes, simple.

This guide is meant to share all of the tips and tricks that I have learned over the years through extensive research and study as well as hands-on experience styling women one-on-one. With this guide, you **will** get your style back. I want to empower you to be the best version of yourself every day, no matter where you are in life, and that starts with self-care and style.

The term self-care is something that gets tossed around quite a bit these days. It's not something I tout lightly. It's very important and directly connected to your style. I believe that **style IS self-care.**

When you look good, you feel good. You are more confident in your personal style, and in yourself. You will be happier, lighter and more joyful!

> **With this guide, you will get your style back.**

By the end of this guide, I want you to be able to answer the following questions:

01. How do you want to present yourself to the world?

02. What is your body shape and style type?

03. How should you dress to complement your body shape?

04. Do you have a signature style?

05. What outfit combination makes you feel the most confident?

06. What wardrobe basics do you need?

07. What steps can you take to dress the body you have today?

While my guide will get you on the right path, ultimately, you should do what is right for you. Don't be afraid to tailor these recommendations to meet your lifestyle, body, and budget. There will be images along the way to help illustrate what I mean, and be sure to watch for spaces where you can write down any answers that pertain to you.

This is *your* book; make it work for you. As you go through this page by page, answer my questions, and figure out your own style, you are creating your best, personalized shopping guide. At the end, you'll be able to head to the store with confidence, knowing exactly what you want to look for and where to find it.

That's my promise.
Erin xo

Getting Started

PART 1

01

Confusion

There's SO much information out there. From trends to body shapes to fast fashion. Not only are there trends, but there are trends within trends (called microtrends). We are left feeling overwhelmed and unsure of our decisions when we try to take it all in.

Does this apply to you? If so, write a few sentences to explain how you feel, and why you feel that way.

Cost

"We have champagne tastes," I love to say, "but we're on a beer budget." If you are on a tight budget, don't fear. There are a bunch of ways you can still dress the way you want. In this guide, I'll show you how to be more strategic. I'll also walk you through my favorite shopping tips to help you save money!

Does this apply to you? If so, write a few sentences to explain how you feel, and why you feel that way.

Time

As women, we juggle jobs, houses, pets, kids, husbands, aging parents, laundry, cleaning, carpooling, schedules, and more. Time is precious. I want you to have your style, but make it work without demanding too much time. Guess what? We can do that.

Does this apply to you? If so, write a few sentences to explain how you feel, and why you feel that way.

ERIN BUSBEE | **STYLE MADE SIMPLE**

Life

Things happen that derail our style, just like with our exercise plans, resolutions, or schedules. Babies, moving to a new town where everyone dresses more casually, changing from a conservative, corporate job to a more laid-back office—these life changes are major and easily throw off your style game.

Does this apply to you? If so, write a few sentences to explain how you feel, and why you feel that way. _____

_____
_____
_____
_____
_____
_____
_____

Age

Transitioning from your twenties to thirties is one difficult period. Many women are often no longer sure what to wear and what is age appropriate. Going from your thirties to your forties is similar. With your body changes, you never want your style to seem desperate—or like you are trying too hard to recapture your youth.

Does this apply to you? If so, write a few sentences to explain how you feel, and why you feel that way. _____

_____
_____
_____
_____
_____
_____

Guilt

This challenge is a big deal for most of us. Growing up Catholic, I have a deep understanding of guilt. If you are Catholic, you'll know exactly what I mean. Maybe you feel like you don't deserve to take care of yourself, or buy that new dress, or splurge on a new wardrobe. Guilt is a very real challenge that so many women take on—and we just don't need to.

Does this apply to you? If so, write a few sentences to explain how you feel, and why you feel that way. _____

_____
_____
_____
_____
_____
_____

Fear

Some of the women I've worked with in the past are afraid to try something new. They really don't want to step outside of their style comfort zone. They just don't know what to do and become paralyzed by fear. We can easily dissipate that fear by learning concrete tips and information. I think you'll find the fear drifts away when you start implementing the changes outlined in this style guide.

Does this apply to you? If so, write a few sentences to explain how you feel, and why you feel that way.

_____
_____
_____
_____
_____
_____
_____
_____
_____

Many of us face one or more of these challenges, which make looking our best feel almost impossible. Through this guide, you'll gain the tools you need so that, regardless of what life throws your way, you can be your most stylish self.

THE BOTTOM LINE IS THIS: *You are not alone!*

> **It's time for you to figure out who you are again.**

style CHALLENGES

My client reached out, caressing the sleeve of a shirt in her closet, then let her arm fall to her side. We stood in front of her closet together, gazing at a haphazard collection of clothing that seemed to be pieced together with half-hearted energy. Her brow furrowed. "I just . . . I don't know what my style is. I don't wear half of this, and the other half doesn't fit. I'm . . . SO lost."

She fidgeted with the bottom of her shirt while her teeth worried her bottom lip. For a moment, her lips moved, wordless. Tears blotched her cheeks.

"It's okay," I said. "You've put everyone else's needs and wants ahead of your own for a long time. It's time for you to figure out who you are again. We'll get through all these challenges together. It's okay to take care of *you* now."

Women tend to think that fashion is selfish, or frivolous and not important. When we're busy taking care of everyone else *but* ourselves, what we're going to wear gets put on the back burner.

I have often heard, "How can I worry about what I look like when I have so much to do?". Kids, partners, careers—we let all of these take front-and-center. Then we deteriorate. We forget who we are, what makes us feel good, and what we like to wear. That leads us to a free-for-all when we go to the store, grabbing anything that sort-of fits, is cheap, or that looked good on someone else.

The truth is this: your style is more about self-care than fashion. It's very important. When you know your style, *you know what you want*. You take the time to look, study, and figure it out. It means that you're making yourself a priority, and that impacts everything.

The other truth is this: When you take the time to care for yourself, you have more to give. You're a better wife, mom, sister, partner, and friend.

The first step on your style journey with this guide is to acknowledge that *your* style challenges actually impede us from becoming our best self and giving our best to those we love. Most of the women I've worked with struggle with the same things that I've listed below.

I've provided space for you to explore which challenges you face. You may find that you struggle with one, three, or *all* of these. Don't be afraid to get real with yourself as you read through them, and answer the questions honestly.

body SHAPES

This style guide is going to be your best companion when you go shopping next, so let's get started with the basics.

Now that you've identified your greatest challenges and started working through them, the next step is to identify your own body shape.

Grab your tape measure—you're going to need it. This may not seem like the fun part, but it's crucial to know your numbers. Once you know your measurements, finding your sizes will be SO much easier. You will also be able to dress in a way that fits and flatters *your body.*

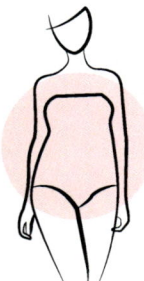 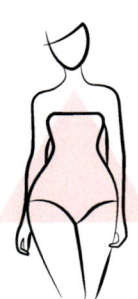 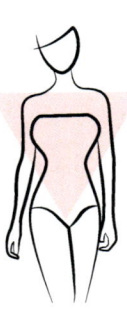 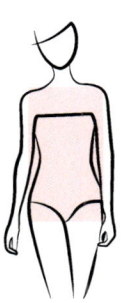 

body MEASUREMENTS

The best part of knowing your measurements is the power it gives you when you are shopping online. Once you know your key measurements, all you have to do to find out the best size is to look at the size chart. Unfortunately, size varies quite a bit between clothing brands. Even within a specific brand or designer, sizes can be all over the place! Knowing your measurements can save a lot of time and aggravation because you won't order clothing online and have to send it back. This guide will ensure that you have quick measurements at the ready, so you know your size for any piece you are ordering!

Where To Measure	Your Measurements
SHOULDERS	
BUST	
WAIST	
HIPS	

Keep these for future!

Shoulders

You want to take this all the way around the width of the shoulders. Put the tape measure on the top of your shoulder so it's almost falling off, then stretch it across your shoulder to the other side. Record the measurement in the box provided above.

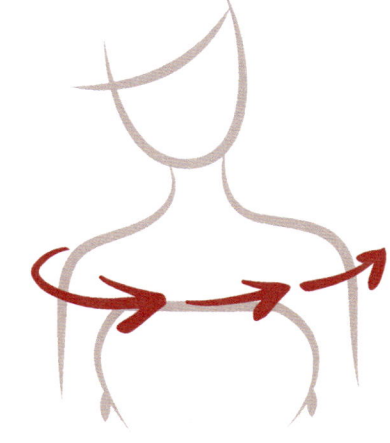

Bust

Take this all the way around the fullest part of your bust. You can wear a lightly padded bra while you're making this measurement. If doing this yourself, bring the tape measure together in front of you for an accurate reading. Record the measurement in the box provided on the previous page.

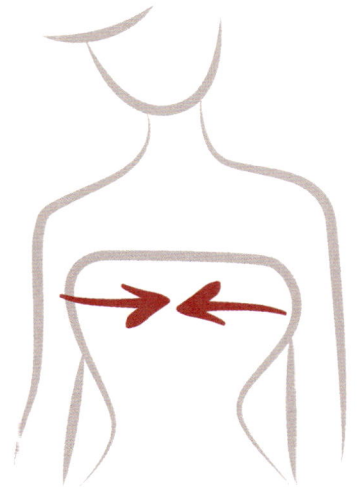

Waist

This is the tiniest part of your natural waist (usually around the belly button). Wrap the tape measure around in front of you for an accurate reading, then record the measurement in the box.

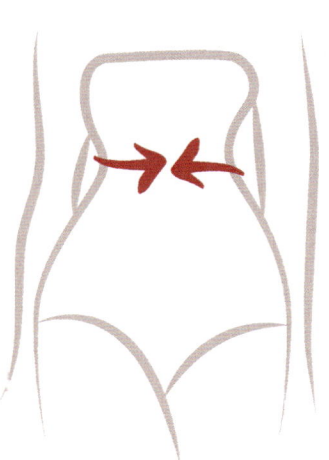

Hips

This is the fullest part of your hips and butt area. Wrap the tape measure around that fullest area for your hips (make sure it doesn't droop in the back), then record the number in the box provided.

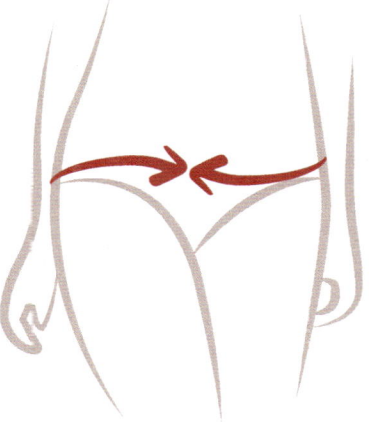

Notes

well-fitting BRA

Don't underestimate the power of a great fitting bra. It will not only defy gravity, lifting your bust up, it will also make you look slimmer and better in clothing. Make sure that you have a great, supportive, uplifting bra. If you haven't had a bra fitting in a while, go into a department store and ask to see a bra fit specialist. Most major department stores have one. Have them fit you, and then see if you know what your size actually is. Remember, something as simple as losing or gaining five pounds can affect your bra size.

You can also take your own measurements to figure out your bra size, but I don't recommend it. Even one slightly wrong measurement can dramatically alter your size. I strongly suggest you make that appointment with a fit specialist and find perfect bras during that appointment (not later). I would aim to buy a smooth and comfortable nude bra, black bra and at least one strapless bra.

My Last Known Bra Size	Bras I Need

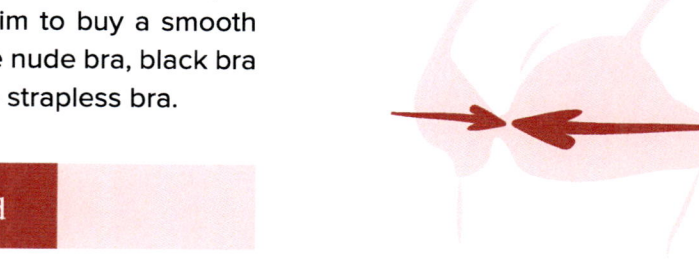

Inverted Triangle

This is an upside-down triangle. With this shape, your shoulders and/or your bust measurement are larger than your hip measurement by about 5%. (Bust is 4+ inches larger. Shoulders are 2+ inches larger.)

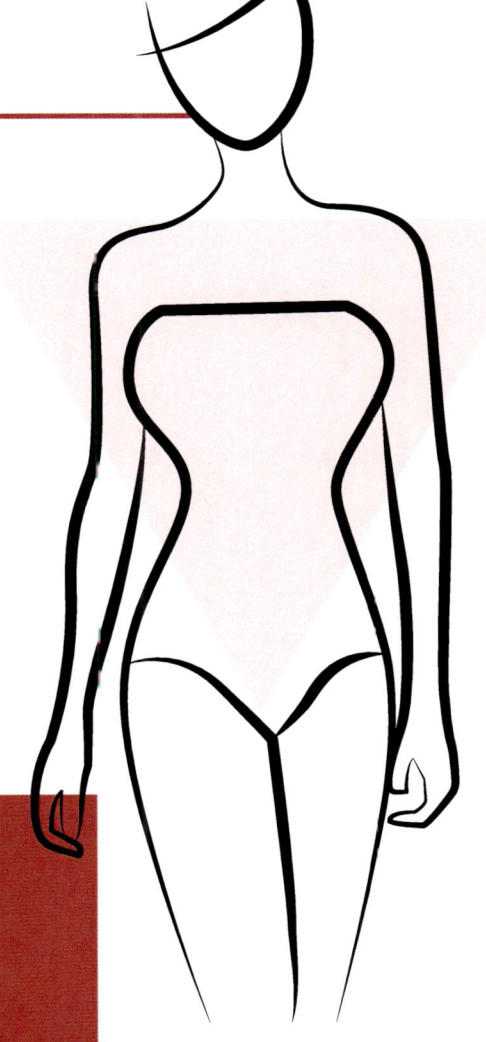

What to do

With the inverted triangle, put all of the pizzazz on the lower half. Wear bold colors and patterns on your lower body to add volume on the lower half and create visual balance. You can also wear A-line skirts and dresses to achieve the same effect.

Minimize your upper body by wearing v-neck or scoop tops and tees, as well as solid colors.

Play up your slim legs and hips by wearing skirts, skinny jeans, tapered trousers, shorts, etc.

Wear v-neck or scoop neck tops and tees to make your upper body appear longer and leaner.

Think about minimizing your upper body by wearing neutral, solid tops and tees.

If your shoulders are broader than your hips, I would consider avoiding shoulder-building details like pleats and pads.

Add volume to your lower body by wearing prints, bold colors and A-line skirts and dresses.

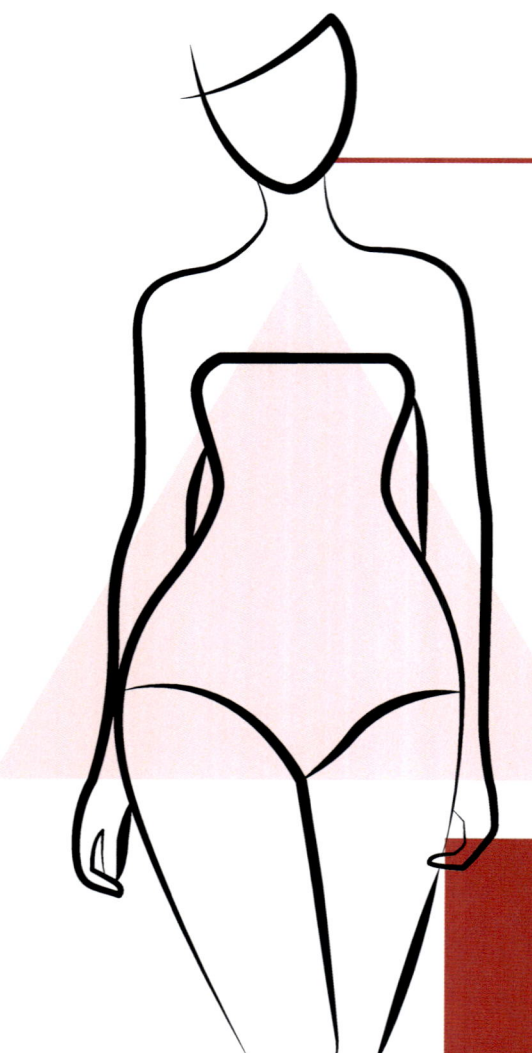

Triangle

Also commonly referred to as pear-shaped, this is the most common body type for women. With this shape, your hip measurement is going to be larger than your bust and shoulders. (Hips are 2+ inches larger than shoulders. Hips are 4+ inches larger than bust.)

What to do

With the triangle shape, think about putting your prints and your bold colors on the top versus the bottom. Avoid lighter jeans and pants on the bottom, and wear lighter colors on the top. Remember that lighter colors, brighter colors, patterns, and metallics are all going to call attention, so place them strategically.

Minimize hips, butt, and thighs by wearing dark, solid colors on your lower body.
Create visual balance by adding color or prints to your upper body.
It may seem counterintuitive, but A-line skirts and dresses pull double duty. They can either add volume or minimize. For triangle types, they minimize.
Wear statement jewelry close to your face to draw the eye up.
Bootcut, straight, and flared jeans will balance out your hips, butt, and thighs. (Skinny jeans create an ice cream cone effect.)

Rectangle

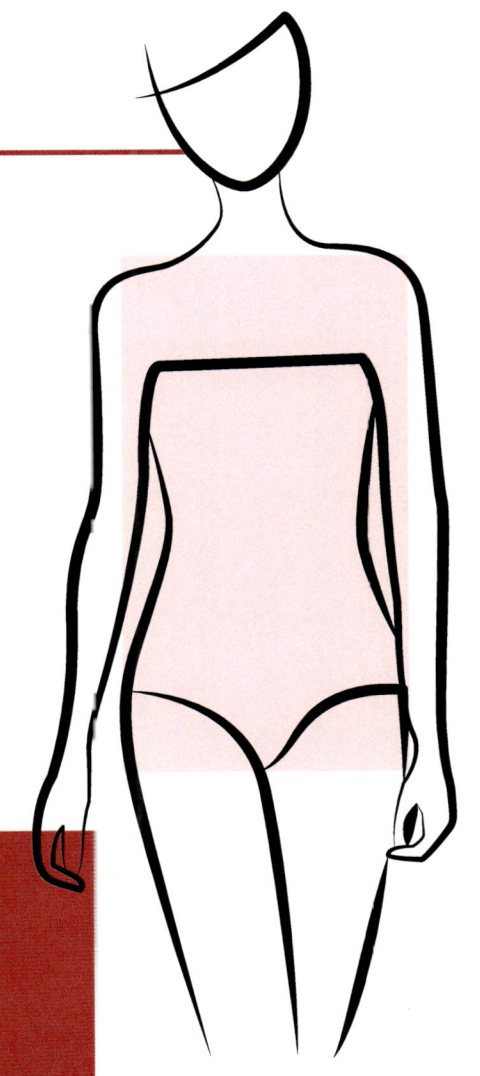

With this shape, your body is straight up and down, with pretty even measurements. That doesn't mean your waist is exactly even to your hips, your bust, and your shoulders. It just means it's not going to be very defined. If your waist nips in less than eight inches from your hips, bust, and shoulders, you are likely a rectangle. This is my body shape.

What to do

Do what Spongebob does and wear pants with a belt! A waist belt creates the illusion of a more defined waist. Waist-defining details like ruching, wraps, a color-blocked panel, or a sheer panel, will also create an illusion of a waist

Consider shoulder-building details to create more visual width across the top, like a puffed shoulder or shoulder pads. Flared and A-line skirts and dresses can also create volume on your lower body.

Create the illusion of a waist by wearing a waist belt.
High-waisted jeans can also create a waist.
A-line skirts and dresses can create more volume on your lower body and make it look like your waist is more defined.
Add shoulder-building details to your look to create more of a curvy shape, such as puff-shoulders and shoulder pads.

Hourglass

With the hourglass shape, your waist is significantly defined. The bust, shoulder, and hip measurements are pretty much the same, but the waist measurement is nipped in, eight or more inches, so you have a clearly defined waist.

What to do

If you're an hourglass shape, go for a tailored and fitted wardrobe that highlights what you already have. Women that carry a little extra weight in their tummy can wear body skimming tops such as loose blouses and tunics that hug curves in a flattering way. Consider an empire waist or ruching in the middle that will mask the tummy area but also highlight it at the same time. High-rise jeans will also help.

Accentuate your tiny waist by wearing a waist belt.
High-waisted jeans will help embrace your curves and highlight your waist.
Wear pencil skirts or any body-hugging dress silhouettes.
Remember that small scale prints like polka dots will make you look smaller and slimmer all over.
Bootcut, straight, and flared pants and jeans will balance out your curvy body. Skinny jeans will emphasize curves.
If you have a little extra weight in the tummy area, define the waist with wrap tops (or faux wrap tops) and ruching that provide forgiveness in that area while still defining the waist.

Circle

With this shape, your waist measurement is larger than your bust, shoulders, or hips by about 5%. (Waist is 2+ inches greater than other measurements.)

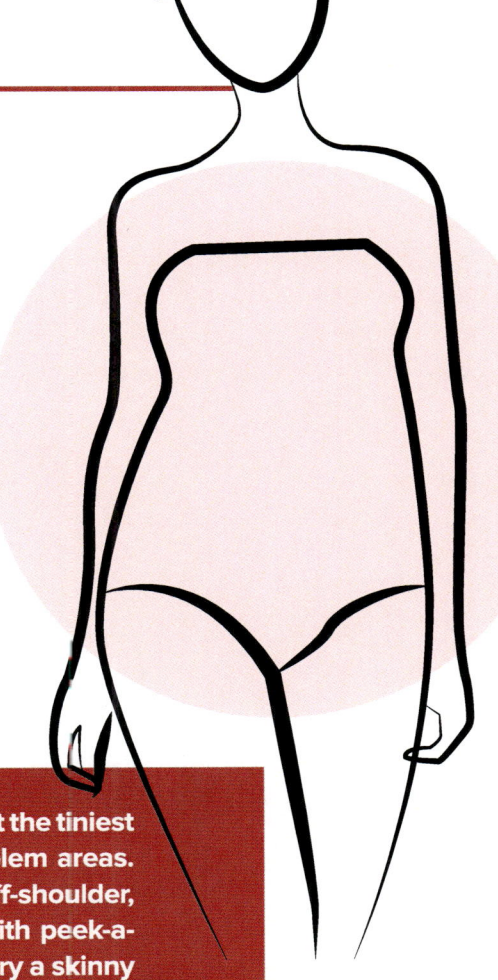

This is the most challenging body shape to dress. You should highlight the tiniest part of your body to maximize your assets and minimize your problem areas. For example, if it's your collarbone/chest area, wear one-shoulder, off-shoulder, v-necks, or cold shoulder tops. (Cold shoulder tops are the ones with peek-a-boo cutouts at the shoulders.) Play around with different tops, then try a skinny jean, legging, Bermuda short, pencil skirt, or something that's streamlined on the bottom if you're doing something a little flowery on the top.

High-waisted jeans will help minimize your tummy area and suck in loose skin and belly fat.
Looser fitting tunic tops that skim the body are a go-to for you.
Create the illusion of a more defined waist by wearing wrap or faux wrap tops, a front-knot detail, or blouses/tees with ruching around the tummy area. They provide forgiveness and definition.
Look for empire waist tops and dresses to highlight the tinier area right under your bust.
Bootcut, straight, and flared pants and jeans will balance out your tummy area.
Wear statement jewelry around your face to draw the eye up and away.
Add a third layer like a cardigan, jacket, or blazer to slim sides and tummy area.
Consider an eye-catching neckline like a v-neck, scoop neck, which will slim your torso and also draw the eye away from your tummy.
Peplum tops can smooth out a tummy area (when they fit correctly).
Structured jackets and tops/sweaters in a weighty fabric like ponte knit will help smooth lumps and bumps.

long vs SHORT-WAISTED

There is one easy and simple way to determine if you're long or short-waisted, which has a huge impact on your style. Take your hands with the palms facing your body and stack them directly underneath your bust. Where does your second hand hit? If your pinky or your hand overlaps your belly button, you're a little bit short-waisted. If you have room before you get to your belly button, you're long-waisted.

What to do

● LONG-WAISTED

If you have a *longer torso*, you want to shorten your upper body and lengthen your lower body. If you're long-waisted, go for higher rise jeans and pants to lengthen legs and cropped jackets or shirt to shorten the torso.

SHORT-WAISTED ●

If you have a *short upper body* with longer legs, you want to make your legs look a little bit shorter and your upper body a little bit longer. That's so easy to do! Simply wear a longer top or jacket and a midrise pair of pants or jeans. It's worth noting that having longer legs and a shorter torso is actually a great look. You can play up your legs by wearing high-rise pants and jeans and tucking in your tops.

Knowledge is power. The more you understand your body, the more confident and empowered you feel getting dressed every morning. Once you're armed with information about your body, you can also easily do additional research on how to dress for your body shape.

With that information comes the ability to make choices that fit and flatter your body, maximize your assets, and minimize your problem areas. Figure out your tiniest part, then highlight it with design details, color, or print. Or you can minimize your problem areas with darker colors, solid colors, no prints, and great tailoring.

Body Shape
What is your body shape?

Waist
Are you long-waisted or short-waisted?

Assets
What are your favorite parts of your body?

What to Do
How will you minimize your problem areas?

ERIN BUSBEE | **STYLE MADE SIMPLE**

style TYPE

Identifying your style type is key to fashion success—almost as important as knowing your body shape. Like it or not, when you meet someone new, they decide within ten seconds, before you even speak, whether you are trustworthy, successful, and confident. Great style makes that solid impression for you!

When you have a better sense of your style, you know how you want to present yourself to the world, how you want to be, and who you are. That is incredibly powerful! (See? Fashion isn't frivolous.)

After all my years styling clients, I've identified categories that can help you determine your style type. I've listed them in the next few pages with a brief explanation for each.

Note: These categories are just jumping off points. They don't necessarily mean you're relegated to one category or boxed in. This framework can help you cherry pick and identify your style type (or types). The importance is providing you a place to start.

Before we continue through the explanations, here's a quick exercise to help you figure out your style type. Think of three words that describe your style. For example, my three words are sophistication, elegance, and edgy. I consider myself to be in both classic and fashion-forward categories, or as I like to call it *edgy elegance.*

Write your three words in the space provided. It may be tricky to keep it to just three, but try to do it. It forces you to pick the ones that *really matter* the most.

I would describe my style as:

_____

_____

_____

Now that you've figured that out (and it isn't always easy!) let's go through the style types.

> **Identifying your style type is key to fashion success.**

ERIN BUSBEE | STYLE MADE SIMPLE

CLASSIC

TIMELESS | MINIMAL | SLEEK

If you like clean lines, minimal details, and timeless pieces that are never going to go out of style, you are drawn to this style. The classic style is no fuss or muss, like Angelina Jolie.

ROMANTIC

FEMININE | SOFT | ELEGANT

This is the super girly look. With a romantic style, you tend to like ruffles, lace, pastels, floral prints, heels, and fit-and-flare dresses. This style type encompasses everything feminine.

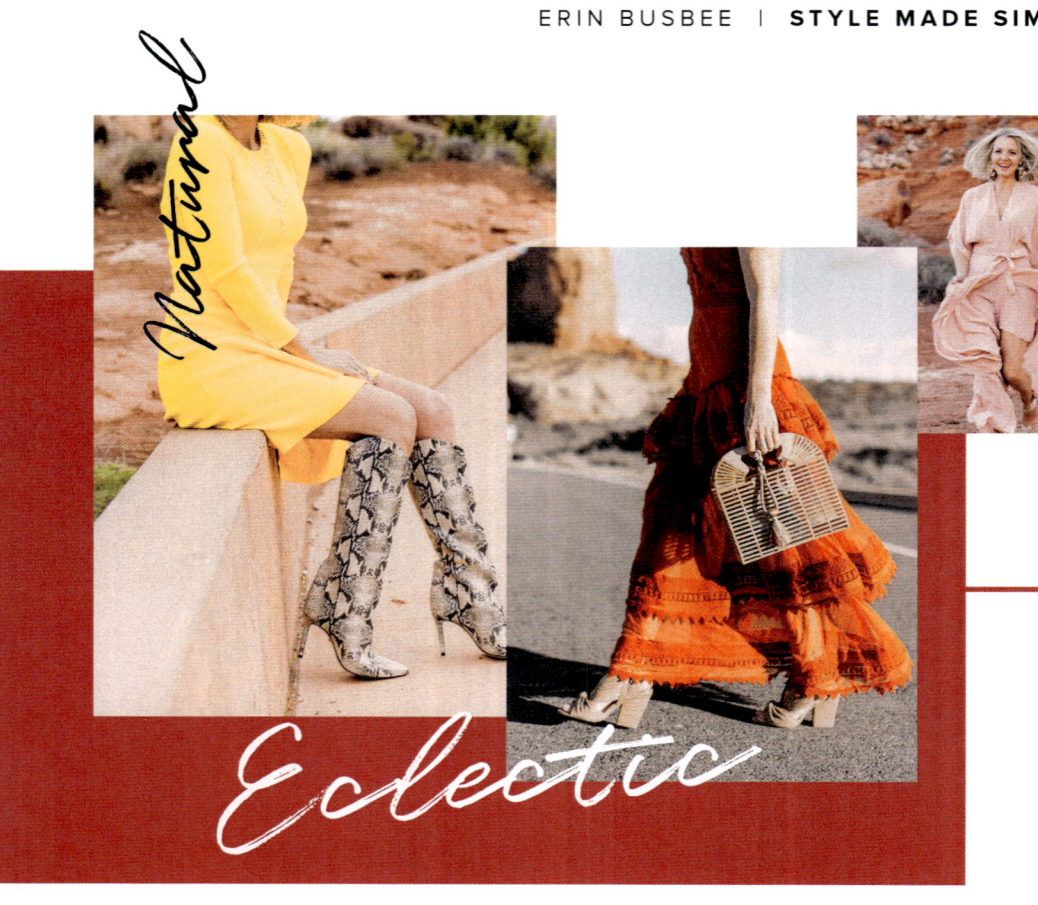

BOHEMIAN
ECLECTIC | NATURAL | FLUID

This is typically somebody that loves fringe, tassels, flowy dresses and skirts, maxi skirts, maxi dresses, flared pants, and jeans — all the styles that were popular in the late sixties and seventies, including round sunglasses and flowy hair.

PREPPY
COLORFUL | NAUTICAL | TAILORED

Do you love to shop at J.Crew and Vineyard Vines? This style is for you! The preppy dresser wears ribbon belts, polo shirts, and chinos. My preppy ladies might feel at home at Martha's Vineyard or Nantucket.

ERIN BUSBEE | STYLE MADE SIMPLE

FASHION FORWARD

MODERN | EDGY | TRENDY

If you're fashion-forward, you might identify or admire celebrities like Gwen Stefani or Rihanna. The fashion-forward woman is a trend-setter who is always taking fashion risks and stays ahead of the trends.

As mentioned before, don't feel restricted to one specific category. You can cross lines and enjoy a few different styles. For example, if I wear feminine pieces, I usually add an edgy piece to offset the femininity. If I wear classic pieces, I add an accessory or a jacket to add excitement and edge to the look.

Beware of style schizophrenia. That's a disorder I made up based on what I saw in many clients' closets. For example, one woman may see a bohemian dress on a friend and think to herself, "I have to have that dress!" So she buys it, and then the dress just hangs in the closet, unworn for years. The reason is because it's not her style. Never buy something just because it looks amazing on someone else. Think about your body shape and your style type. Does the purchase make sense for you?

Knowing your style type saves precious time, money, and energy. Your closet doesn't fill up with items you're not going to wear. You stay on track and on target while you're shopping. It truly helps your personality shine through because you are wearing pieces that really represent the person you are and the person you want to be.

When you know yourself and your style, it's easier to get dressed, to style your clothes, and to shop. Remember, your style is an expression of you. It encompasses who you are.

Your style is you.

Look & Feel
How do you want to look and feel when you step out the door?

Style
What style type(s) do you think would help you feel most comfortable and confident?

Notes
Anything else that has sparked your interest or has been thought provoking.

If you need to see some of these tips in action, you can check out my style tutorials geared for women over 40 on my YouTube channel, *Busbee Style.*

02
Getting Detailed
—— PART 2 ——

Wardrobe Basics, Section I

Now that you've made it into Part Two, you've come a long way. Way to go! You've taken your measurements, reviewed your body shape, and established your style type (or types). Now that we have a great foundation, we're ready to dive a bit deeper into the details.

In Part Two, we're going to review the details of your style (and your closet) and really focus on building your confidence. The first step is making sure you have all the basics in your wardrobe.

the capsule WARDROBE

Like your home, your wardrobe needs a solid foundation. That foundation are your basics. Without that, you can't build. When I worked with clients, 99% of the time the issue they came to me with was the lack of basics. They simply didn't have the necessary foundation pieces I speak about so often. That's why they struggled to put outfits together day after day.

What ends up happening for most of us when we shop is that we're attracted to the shiny, and the bright, and the bold, and the pretty, or the trendy. We want something new and fun, but we overlook and forget those basic pieces. They play an integral role in our wardrobes. Put another way, if you don't have them, your wardrobe won't work.

Go through the wardrobe basics checklists on the following pages carefully. Just because you may check off that you have skinny jeans and dark jeans doesn't mean they're current! Be really honest with yourself. Here are a few questions to answer as you consider each piece:

Does it *fit* my body?

Do I *want* to wear it?

Is this item *current?*

Does it *flatter* my body?

Do I feel *comfortable* in it?

Once you have these basics covered, you can add in color, fun prints, sparkle, glitter, and anything you want because you know you have the foundation pieces necessary to pair with these others.

WARDROBE BASICS

spring & summer

Tops & Swim

- [ ] White button-up
- [ ] White cotton top or blouse
- [ ] White silky, elegant blouse
- [ ] Black and white short-sleeved tees
- [ ] Black and white long-sleeved tees
- [ ] Two printed or solid color blouses
- [ ] One cardigan
- [ ] One swimsuit, coverup, and sunhat

Undergarments

- [ ] Black and nude strapless bras
- [ ] Black and nude smooth or t-shirt bras
- [ ] Black and nude skirt slip
- [ ] (One with tummy control!)
- [ ] Nippes or NuBra

Dresses & Skirts

- [ ] White and black dress
- [ ] Printed or solid summer dress
- [ ] Black and white skirt (any style)

Pants

- [ ] Dark wash skinny jeans
- [ ] Dark wash bootcut or flared jeans
- [ ] Flattering black trousers (wide-leg)
- [ ] Black ankle trousers, tapered
- [ ] Black leggings
- [ ] One pair of denim shorts
- [ ] One pair of black, navy, or white shorts
- [ ] Cropped pants or jeans

Outerwear & Bags

- [ ] Perfect black blazer (one button, hip-length)
- [ ] White jacket or blazer
- [ ] Lightweight jacket (neutral color)
- [ ] Leather jacket
- [ ] Black, tan, or navy trench coat
- [ ] Black or metallic clutch (day-to-night)
- [ ] Black or honey brown cross-body bag
- [ ] Black or honey brown shoulder bag

Shoes & Sandals

- [ ] Black, nude, or metallic flats (closed-toe)
- [ ] Black or nude pumps
- [ ] Statement heels
- [ ] Nude or metallic sandals
- [ ] Black sandals
- [ ] One pair of wedges or heeled sandals
- [ ] Flip flops or easy on/off shoes (for beach or pool)

Accessories

- [ ] Silk/dressy scarf
- [ ] Statement accessory (solid or multi-color)
- [ ] Everyday gold and silver necklace
- [ ] Everyday gold and silver bracelet
- [ ] Everyday gold and silver earrings
- [ ] Everyday gold and silver ring
- [ ] Black and brown sunglasses
- [ ] Reversible belt

fall & winter
WARDROBE BASICS

Tops & Sweaters

- [ ] Black and white camisoles
- [ ] Black and white long-sleeved tees
- [ ] Two great quality sweaters
- [ ] One black turtleneck or knit top sweater
- [ ] One cardigan (hip length)
- [ ] White or ivory blouse or button-up
- [ ] Two solid color blouses

Pants & Dresses

- [ ] Dark wash skinny jeans
- [ ] Dark wash bootcut or flared jeans
- [ ] Flattering black trousers (wide-leg)
- [ ] Black ankle trousers, tapered
- [ ] Black leggings
- [ ] Black skirt (silhouette to flatter your body)
- [ ] Black denim
- [ ] Two versatile black dresses

Undergarments

- [ ] Black and nude strapless bras
- [ ] Black and nude smooth bras
- [ ] Black and nude skirt slip (tummy control!)
- [ ] Nudge thigh shaper spanx
- [ ] Black opaque stockings
- [ ] Black patterned tights/stockings
- [ ] Nippes or NuBra

Boots & Shoes

- [ ] Black pumps
- [ ] Black booties
- [ ] Black or honey knee-high boots
- [ ] Ballet flats
- [ ] Snow boots (climate dependent)
- [ ] Statement shoes
- [ ] Metallic or black evening shoes
- [ ] Rain boots

Outerwear & Bags

- [ ] Perfect black blazer (one button, hip-length)
- [ ] Black or tan trench coat
- [ ] Black or camel wool coat
- [ ] Black puffer coat (climate dependent)
- [ ] Leather jacket (black most versatile)
- [ ] Black or metallic clutch (day-to-night)
- [ ] Black or honey brown cross-body bag
- [ ] Black or honey brown shoulder bag

Accessories

- [ ] Warm scarf and silky/dressy scarf
- [ ] Neutral gloves and hat (climate dependent)
- [ ] Everyday gold and silver necklace
- [ ] Everyday gold and silver bracelet
- [ ] Everyday gold and silver earrings
- [ ] Everyday gold and silver ring
- [ ] Black and brown sunglasses
- [ ] Reversible belt

The basics on the previous pages are based on a black-gold palette. If you prefer, you can choose a navy and beige or tan color palette.

After going through this list, what have you found? Are you missing a few items? Chances are good that you have a few things to buy—and that's the fun part! I've provided space below for you to write out the pieces you need to shop for on your next outing. This can be assembled over time. Don't feel like you have to have it all in one shopping trip.

Shopping list

Now that we have the basics established for your closet (as well as a great head start on what you need to stock up on for your next shopping trip!), let's go a little deeper. Not only do I want you to have this wardrobe, but I want you to find the right pieces that fit and flatter your body. Don't just check a box. Make sure those basics are pieces you love and pieces that make you feel confident.

In this next section, I'm going to tackle the basics in more detail, and tell you exactly how they should be worn. The small details may not seem important, but they really step up your style game.

trouser HEMLINE

For a traditional, wide, or straight-leg trouser, the bottom of the pant leg should almost dust the floor. It should be **one-half to three-quarters of an inch** off the ground, showing just a sliver of your shoes. This length will create the most professional, polished, elongating, slimming look. And it's surprisingly hard to find! When I do professional, corporate speaking events, I have to search through the crowd to find someone that's done it correctly!

Part of the problem with the right trouser length is our shoes. If you have a pair of trousers that you love, but you want to wear different shoes with it, all you need to do is own two pairs of those pants with different hemline lengths. You own one pair of pants for your favorite pair of pumps or heels, and then you get the other pair for your flats, loafers, or a lower-heeled shoe.

The proportion of the pant is surprisingly important, and it has a big impact on your overall look. This is one of the most common fashion mistakes that I see.

> Do you have any trousers that you could hem (or take to a tailor)? List them here for easy identification later.

_____   _____   _____
_____   _____   _____
_____   _____   _____

> Do you need to invest in different heel heights or flats to pair with your existing pants? List those below.

_____   _____   _____
_____   _____   _____
_____   _____   _____

skirt LENGTH

When it comes to your skirt in a professional setting, I strongly suggest that you keep the hemline in the knee zone. I made that up—basically it means to have your hemline a little above your knee, at the knee, or a little below. This will keep you looking the most polished and the most professional. It's a fail-safe hemline length for the office.

What skirts do you own that fit and flatter you?

_____ _____ _____
_____ _____ _____
_____ _____ _____

What skirts would you like to invest in?

_____ _____ _____
_____ _____ _____
_____ _____ _____

Do you have any skirts that need tailoring (hem into knee zone) or dry cleaning? List them here for easy identification later.

_____ _____ _____
_____ _____ _____

blazer BASICS

The blazer is a key piece in your professional wardrobe. It's a jacket with long sleeves, lapels, and either gold or silver buttons. It can be worn alone, casually, or more formally. When you're looking for a great blazer, one that you can wear all the time, fit is really important. Let's dive into making sure your blazer is the exact right fit for you.

SHOULDERS
The first thing that needs to fit properly are the shoulders. If the seam is toward the outside of your shoulder, you might want to look at petite sizing, or take the blazer to the tailor and have the seam cheated in. This is important, because when your shoulder seams are too wide, your sleeve length will be too long, and your shoulders may look slumped.

BLAZER TYPE
For maximum versatility, I would invest first in a one-button blazer that follows the natural curves of your body. It shouldn't gather, pucker, or bunch up in any part of the torso or near the shoulders.

SLEEVE AND BLAZER HEMLINE
A fail-safe length for the blazer is to make sure it falls at the hip bone. Find your hip bone—or where your hip and leg joint meet—you want to keep your blazer hemline there.

Longer blazers called longline or boyfriend blazers are very on trend right now. I happen to love them, but they are not as versatile as a hip length blazer. They can also elongate your upper body. That works well for those of you with long torsos. If you are petite, those blazers can cut off your legs.

With a full-length sleeve, the length should be somewhere between the wrist and your first thumb joint. If you opt for a three-quarter sleeve blazer, keep in mind that where the sleeve falls is where the eye will go. That usually means the tummy area.

If you are very busty and struggle to find a blazer that fits you, look for softer knit blazers or swap a blazer for a cardigan sweater. You can also find a piece that fits you in the shoulders and bust and have the waist taken in.

What blazers do you own?

_____   _____   _____
_____   _____   _____

Do your blazers fall above or below your hip bone? List them here for easy identification later.

_____   _____   _____
_____   _____   _____

Slimming Tricks

Next are styling tricks to make you look slimmer. These tricks obviously won't magically take pounds off your body, but they can create the illusion that you've lost ten pounds. It's referred to sometimes as **thinner by dinner.**

I love these tricks! I use them all the time. After I had both kids, I used them immediately after their births. People would say to me all the time, "How'd you lose the weight so quickly?" It was all style smoke and mirrors.

Shapewear

Shapewear is an extra step that can make you look a lot thinner, especially under a more fitted dress or skirt. It helps smooth everything out and removes lumps and bumps. I really love shapewear slips that are like skirts. They really suck everything in while still allowing a little freedom for the potty. 😉 The high-rise briefs were especially helpful after having kids because it sucks in the tummy area and makes your waist sometimes two to three inches smaller.

What are you trying to minimize? (i.e. tummy, thighs)

List shapewear you would like to invest in here:

Jean Rise

The rise of your jeans is also important, especially if you have extra weight around the tummy. Let's say you're prone to a muffin top. (That's where excess skin or fat hangs over the top of your jeans.) If this is something you struggle with, consider wearing high-rise jeans. It's a game changer that will trim inches off. When you have a muffin top, and you just wear a top over it, often you can still see the overhang or bumps on the sides. When you wear high-rise jeans, it sucks all that in and makes you appear slimmer and smoother all over. These are a really great trick. High-rise jeans are usually nine inches or higher and go up to your belly button.

Monochromatic Dressing

It's an oldie, but a goody! Monochromatic dressing can be with any color that you want. Simply wear one color from head to toe, and you'll look longer, taller and slimmer. This is one of the most under-utilized tools that we have in our styling toolbox. It doesn't necessarily have to be the exact same color, but similar colors. For example, you can wear a black turtleneck and dark blue jeans. When I wear a monochromatic look, I LOVE to mix tones and textures. (Think angora sweater with leather pants and suede boots as an example.)

> It doesn't necessarily have to be the exact same color, but similar colors.

Dark Jeans

Dark jeans make you appear slimmer, taller, and longer. They are also dressier and more sophisticated than lighter wash jeans, so make sure you have a pair handy to grab when you need them.

> **Dark jeans make you appear thinner.**

Before

After

ERIN BUSBEE | STYLE MADE SIMPLE

Smaller Scale Prints

Wearing smaller scale prints versus larger scale prints can help you appear slimmer. If you wear smaller scale prints (like little itty-bitty polka dots or little hearts), that's going to make you look slimmer.

ERIN BUSBEE | STYLE MADE SIMPLE

Before  *After*

> **Look slimmer, longer, and taller.**

Wide-legged Pants

Wide- or flared-leg pants are going to make you look slimmer, longer, and taller. Whenever I want to look taller than my 5'4" frame, I always pull out a pair of exaggerated wide-leg pants with the highest, most comfortable wedge I can wear. All of a sudden, my legs look like they're a mile long. You can even hide the heels underneath your pants!

Fake Tan

The last trick I want to talk about is the fake tan. It's a great way to make everything look slimmer and more toned. Spray-tan abs anyone? It is another fantastic tool to have in your toolbox.

Before / After

Jewelry

Jewelry can be a strategic part of helping you look slimmer. Put jewelry in places where you want the eye to go because jewelry is eye-catching. If you want the eye to go to your chest, put a really beautiful statement necklace there. If you want the eyes to go to your hands, then wear jewelry on your hands. If you want the eyes drawn to your face, then wear some great statement earrings. You can also wear a long, pendant necklace or long, layered necklaces, which will elongate the upper body. If you have large breasts, you may want to skip longer necklaces.

What jewelry do you need to invest in? Pendant necklace? Earrings?

Fabric Choices

If you wear really thin jersey materials, keep in mind that they can be really unforgiving and may show everything. A structured fabric, like a denim or a neoprene, is going to be more forgiving.

Avoid bulky fabrics. Velvets are really in right now, but be aware that they're going to make you look a little bigger. Brocades, angora or mohair sweaters, leather, and suede can cause this as well. Remember to reflect on the body shape guidelines, and place these heavier fabrics strategically on an area of the body where you prefer to add volume.

ERIN BUSBEE | STYLE MADE SIMPLE

> **Have a go-to pair of nude shoes.**

Skin-tone Shoes

A shoe color that matches your skin tone is definitely elongating. For example, let's say you're wearing a black dress or a floral print dress, and you want your legs to look longer. Wear a nude shoe. "Nude" can be a range. For me, nude is a light beige. For you, it might be a deep cognac. Whatever the color of your skin, have a go-to pair of nude shoes to help you look slimmer and your legs look longer.

What shoes do you have that can lengthen your legs?

Accentuate

When slimming down for a night out, consider highlighting the tiniest part of your body. If you have a small waist, highlight that waist with a belt, a design detail, or a color block panel. Let's say the smallest part of your body is right under your bust. In that case, wear an empire waist top or dress or consider a necklace that drops to under the bust.

What is the smallest part of your body?

How can you highlight it?

---

dressing YOUR AGE

Out of all the things I discuss, this topic tends to be the most controversial. I want to say out of the gate that you can wear whatever you want, whatever makes you feel happiest, whatever makes you feel the most confident, whatever makes you feel the most comfortable. My role is simply to guide you. I'm in no way saying you can't wear this, or you can wear that. We all age... we all change.

With that change often comes style changes. Whether you are transitioning from your twenties to thirties or sliding into your forties and fifties. These different phases of life and age milestones can completely throw off our style game. When we're talking about dressing for your age, I want you to connect with the part of you that asks the question, "Is this appropriate for my age?" That's the voice that you should be listening to. Are you uncomfortable about a piece and asking that question? Or are you genuinely motivated to wear it, but worried what people will say? For me, dressing in a way that is age appropriate comes down to two things: modification and sophistication. Let's go through some general guidelines that will help you overcome some common age-related hurdles.

> **We all age... we all change.**

ERIN BUSBEE | STYLE MADE SIMPLE

Skirt Hemlines

If you want to wear a mini-skirt and you're proud of your legs, wear the mini-skirt! I would, however, go back to the one-skin rule that I discussed previously and make a few modifications. If you're going to show a lot of leg, cover up more on top. If you want to wear a shorter hemline, you could also wear tights. Tights make the look more sophisticated, classic, and a bit more conservative.

Shorts

While there's no rule on shorts (like the mini-skirt)—if you want to wear them and are proud of your legs, do it! Take into account overall sophistication, comfort, and style. When wearing shorts, consider keeping the upper body more covered, with a roll-up sleeve cotton or linen shirt, or maybe a short-sleeved shirt that offers more coverage on your upper body. Adding chic wedges or heels can elevate your look too.

Ripped Jeans

The topic of ripped jeans is another question I get a lot. Can I wear ripped jeans after a certain age? If you want to wear ripped jeans, wear them! Maybe choose a pair that's only mildly distressed. Whatever amount of distressing you chose, try them with a turtleneck or a nice chunky sweater on top to offset the leg exposure. Something more modest and classic on top will also offset the trendiness of the jeans.

ERIN BUSBEE | **STYLE MADE SIMPLE**

Modern Trends

Under no circumstances does aging mean that you can't try modern trends. Pick one trend and then keep everything else pretty classic. For example, if you want to wear a lace-up top, try a lace-up sweater or sweatshirt, simply pair it with classic, dark wash jeans, and call it a day. If you love motorcycle jackets, pair the jacket with a turtleneck or classic blouse and jeans. You do not need to try every trend. Find one or two trends that really speak to you, that you really love, and try them! They key is to pair those trendy pieces with classic basics.

Sizing

Don't get hung up on the size number. Ever heard of vanity sizing? Because of vanity sizing, the numbers are ALL over the place! Sizing varies dramatically from brand to brand, even within brands sometimes. Just make sure the garment fits you, feels comfortable on you, and gives you a little wiggle room. More often than not, if something is a little bit roomy on you, it makes you look skinnier.

Dated Items

Be sure that you don't have anything too dated in your closet because those pieces will potentially make you look older. Trends always come and go, but typically there is a new modification of the trend. and that's why it's not always a great idea to simply bust out your 80's blazers.

Message Tees

This is the kind of clothing that's perfect if you're kicking around the house on the weekend, or you're going to a kid's sports game. On a regular basis, proceed with caution. I know there is a huge message tee trend right now, but do you really need to wear a top or sweater that says "Rosé All Day?" Is that making the best impression? And I would caution against wearing any type of message tee in a professional setting. If you insist on a message tee for higher-level events, keep it on the sophisticated side by wearing a blazer or a tweed jacket over it. That will elevate the tee.

Crop Tops

Crop tops are very on-trend right now. We've been seeing a lot of crop sweaters and crop jackets. In the fall, consider wearing a higher rise pair of pants or jeans with a simple crop top. That way you are not really showing much skin in the mid-section. You can also layer under the crop top, so that you have extra coverage. There are ways you can modify crop tops to make them more appropriate for your age, body, and comfort level. If you don't want to draw attention to your stomach, the crop top isn't the trend or hemline for you.

ERIN BUSBEE | **STYLE MADE SIMPLE**

"Will you own it when you wear it?"

When it comes to dressing for your age, the bottom line is this: make sure it's something you're comfortable wearing, you feel confident in it, and it works well for your body and style. There's no reason why you can't look modern and fresh regardless of your age! You can wear trends; you can try color; you can do prints. You can do all of it. Just make sure you modify and check yourself. Do you really look good in it? Do you feel good in it? Are you comfortable and confident. Most importantly: will you own it when you wear it? ***Confidence is key!***

key styling TIPS FOR YOU

We tackled quite a few styling tips in the Age Appropriate Dressing and Slimming Tricks sections, but there are a few other key styling tips and tricks that are important to share with you. You can put clothes on your body, but the styling is what sets your outfits apart from the crowd and enables you to express your personality.

Your Signature Style

Nothing makes me feel better or like I can tackle the world more than an awesome blazer, fabulous jeans, and heels. It's my armor and what I feel the most confident in. What is your signature style?

If you are unsure, look in your closet and see what you have multiples of. For example, if you see a sea of jackets and striped tops, maybe your signature style is a striped top with an edgy jacket, jeans, and heels. As part of your signature style, consider one special accessory that means something to you. For example, a necklace with your children's birthstones or a bracelet inscribed with your favorite quote. I like to wear a gold necklace with a honeybee pendant for Busbee.

What is your signature style?

_____
_____
_____
_____
_____

ERIN BUSBEE | STYLE MADE SIMPLE

The Hat Effect

Hats can totally change your look in a great way! You can wear a simple combination like jeans, a tee, and when you add a hat, voila! Instant cool factor! That's the hat effect.

The Third Layer

When you want to add polish to your look, add a third layer. That can be a jacket, blazer, vest, duster cardigan, etc. If you live in a hot climate, consider investing in a sheer button-up dress or vest to wear as your third layer. You will also likely need lightweight jackets and blazers for heavily air-conditioned places.

Belts

I get asked all the time, "When should I wear a belt?" The truth is, unless your pants are falling down, you hardly ever need a belt. They are fabulous accessory that can add a lot of pop to your look. Not to mention define your waist! I love to wear belts at my natural waist (belly button) to create a tinier waist. I also love wearing them with high-rise jeans. You can wear a belt over your trench coats or blazers to add some polish and structure to those pieces. Also, don't be afraid to swap the belt that comes with a garment, with your own, more stylish belt. Your belts will always be nicer.

Accessories

My rule of thumb with accessories is to add at least one impactful accessory to your look every day. That can be a belt, hat, necklace, scarf, earrings, etc. One can be enough. If you are going to mix your metals (gold, silver, rose gold) I would invest in an anchor piece. That's an accessory like a necklace that has both gold and silver to tie your metals together. Also keep in mind that you do NOT have to match your handbag to your shoes, but you certainly can match them if you'd like.

Cuff it

I love to cuff button-up shirts. My go-to cuff is the J.Crew cuff, where you fold over the end of your sleeve into one long cuff (like six inches), fold it almost in-half again, leaving just a touch of the end of the sleeve hemline. You can fold back the end of the sleeve a tiny bit. This is much easier to watch, so refer to my video featuring this cuff.

ERIN BUSBEE | **STYLE MADE SIMPLE**

Your Colors

I get asked at least once a week, "How do I know what my colors are?" Here's the thing—every color has a zillion shades. Some shades will work for you and some won't. Think about the shades you wear already that add a little spring to your step. The ones you wear and all of your coworkers, friends, and family, compliment you in. Those are your colors.

The Art of the Tuck

For a more casual outfit, and when you want to highlight your waist, try a half or French tuck for an effortless look. That's when you tuck in part of the front of your top. For more professional looks, I would employ the full tuck.

fashion FIX-ITS

There are many styling issues that arise on a regular basis that you may need solutions to. I call these fashion fix-its. I wanted to share a few of the most important ones so you feel like you are ready for whatever wardrobe malfunction comes your way.

Double-Sided Tape

A wardrobe stylist's number one fashion fix-it is double-sided tape. You can use it to keep excess belt leather from flapping around, fix a floppy jacket lapel, keep your button-up shirt from popping open and exposing too much, hold down a plunging neckline, keep your hemline up, or hold a cuff in place. And so on and so on...

Leather Hole Punch

I buy belts that are always a bit larger so I can wear them around my hips AND around my natural waist, but that means there usually aren't enough holes. I simply grab my leather hole puncher, careful to select the right size hole, and add my own.

Shoe Fixes

If you are having a shoe problem, there IS an answer. There are toe fillers for when the shoe is just a ½ size too big. Heel pads for blister prevention and to prevent slippage. Feet spray to keep feet more comfortable in heels all day. Blister blocker for prevention. Heel covers for occasions when you want to wear heels in grass. Identify your problem in advance (or that you've been noticing), and grab whatever you need to fix it.

Nipple Covers with Lift

I won't pretend nipple covers offer a lot of support, but they are a necessary evil when you have a neckline or open back that you can't quite find the right bra for. I would look for a set of nipple covers that lifts as well as covers so your breasts aren't sagging.

If you need any help—or have other slimming tricks of your own—don't hesitate to pop into my Facebook group and post some pictures, or talk to other women just like you that want some direct feedback. You are not alone on this fashion journey! Sign up to *www.busbeestyle.com/hive*

> **Identify your problem in advance and grab whatever you need to fix it.**

Getting Organized

PART 3

03

closet EDITING

Now that we've not only figured out more about your style (or styles), and worked through your body shape and the basics, let's get you ready for your next big shopping trip. That starts with closet editing.

Closet editing can be kind of tough because there is an emotional component to it that you need to plan for. As women, we get emotionally attached to our clothes for various reasons. Maybe it reminds us of a special experience, or a trip. Maybe we paid a lot of money for it or a super-duper special friend gave it to us. There are innumerable reasons why we hang onto clothes for way too long. The hardest part of the process is just letting go.

I usually do my closet editing at least twice a year. Springtime is a great time to do it, and then I usually do it once in early fall. Consider editing during a time when everyone is out of the house. This is a laborious and emotional process. Give yourself time.

You've heard the statistic—we all wear 20% of our closet 80% of the time. Today, let's try to make your closet more functional and less overwhelming.

So let's dive in with where to start, because what's more overwhelming than a closet full of things you never really wear?

> **Let's get you ready for your next big shopping trip.**

Have a System

The first part of the editing process is to make sure you have a system that will allow you to flip quickly through your clothes and make a decision. For this, I use a portable rolling rack. It allows me to keep pieces hung up and neat, but move through them quickly. You could use your bed or whatever works. I like the rolling rack because then you can really flip through the clothes, look at them, and make a quick and easy decision. It also keeps everything on the hanger, easy to see, and organized.

In addition to your rolling rack, grab garbage bags and plenty of boxes for all those items you decide to purge. The boxes are for shoes and heavier items.

Plan on keeping organized clothing bags. Have a donate bag, a trash bag, a tailoring bag, and a drycleaning bag. If you're cleaning out your drawers and beauty supplies, you can put those in the boxes you set aside, along with the shoes, boots, and bags you plan to donate. These are usually heavy and bulky and easier to cart it out in a box.

Finally, start with one section of your closet at a time. I usually take three feet worth of clothes, (which is about 100 hangers) and go through one type of clothing. For example, I grab all my dresses, then go through each piece individually, using my criteria to determine what stays and what goes.

ERIN BUSBEE | **STYLE MADE SIMPLE**

Closet Editing Criteria

Size and Fit: Ask yourself, "Is this something that I can realistically wear now?" Don't keep anything that doesn't fit you. Get real with yourself. You may have items that you hold onto because you think, "Oh, I want to lose ten pounds so I can wear that someday." I strongly recommend that you get rid of those. You can put them in a box and put them away. When you do lose ten pounds, pull them back out. Your closet shouldn't be a daily reminder of your body goals or your weight goals. Your closet should be an oasis.

Damaged Clothing: If something is worn, faded, stained, damaged, or has holes, you want to throw those out. Nobody's going to want your damaged goods, so don't put them in you donate pile. White shirts tend to get yellowed or lose their brightness. Replenish those white shirts every couple of seasons.

When is the last time I wore this?: Generally speaking, if you haven't worn something in the last two years, you're probably not going to wear it. There may be some exceptions, so pull those pieces out, put them in another closet, and save them for a rainy day. If it's a sentimental piece, like a wedding dress, or suede or leather, put them somewhere else so they're not taking up that prime real estate in your closet.

Special Occasion Dresses: You don't need to keep your special occasion dresses. We all hang on to our special occasion dresses like they're jewels, but they get dated really fast. Ged rid of the ones you're not wearing anymore. There is no reason to hold onto those unless you actually love them and will actually wear them again (and they are classic enough to wear again).

How do I feel?: *A la Marie Kondo.* If you follow along with the Marie Kondo method, you would ask yourself, "Does this bring me joy? Is this joyful?" I like to ask, "Does this make me feel pretty?" If the answer is no, and you don't feel cute or particularly special in it, and it doesn't bring joy or a smile to your face, then get rid of it.

One last thing to remember while closet editing: store off-season pieces somewhere else to create more space in your closet.

Editing your closet is really hard and emotional because of our strong attachments. Think about letting things go in a really positive way. I used to say to clients, let someone else enjoy this beautiful garment. No one is enjoying them if they are just hanging in your closet collecting dust. If you let go of these pieces, then other people can appreciate them, love them, need them, and enjoy them.

When are you going to do your closet editing? SET A DATE.

Are there any supplies you need to buy to get ready?

STYLE MADE SIMPLE

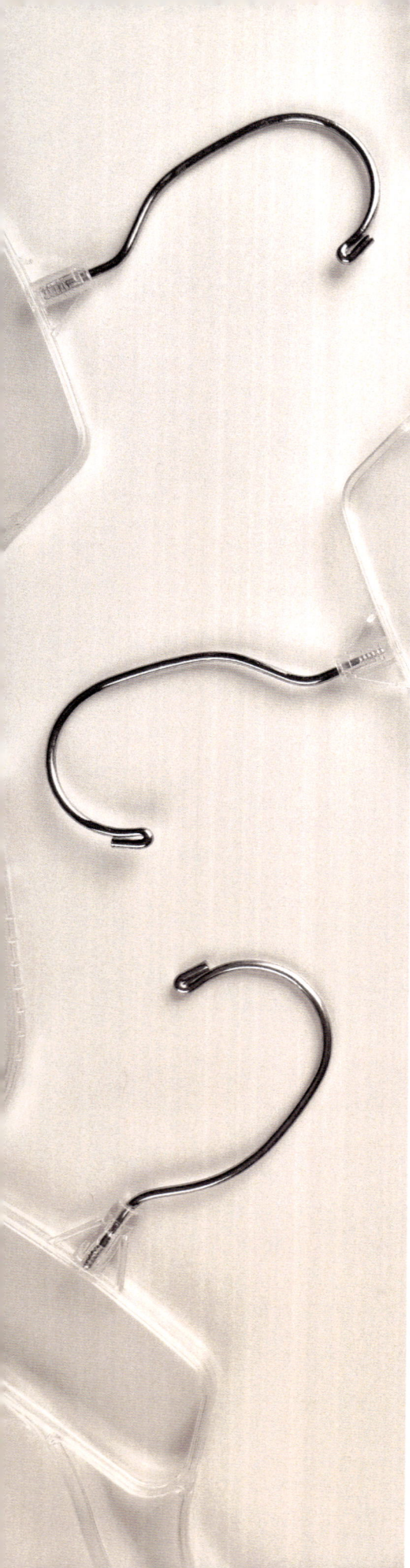

closet ORGANIZATION

I have a love-hate relationship with closet organization. I love the polished, sleek, finished feel of a boutique-like closet, but I hate getting there! (Thankfully, this is far easier to do than closet editing!) The great thing about organizing your closet now is that it will be totally done later, which makes it easier to keep organized as you continue to add or remove clothes from your wardrobe.

Buy Matching Hangers: Matching hangers is an upfront investment that's well worth it. Plan on buying around one hundred hangers for every three feet of full hanging space. Consider buying the plastic, swivel head hangers so that no matter what direction you hang your garment, they face the same way by just adjusting the head.

There may be times when your garment is too wide for the hanger, and it doesn't stay on, which is why some people prefer the velvet, non-slip hangers. You can also waterfall these hangers if you have a really small closet space, or buy containers for one-sleeved dresses or other pieces that will lose shape when hung up.

This type for shirts and for dresses.

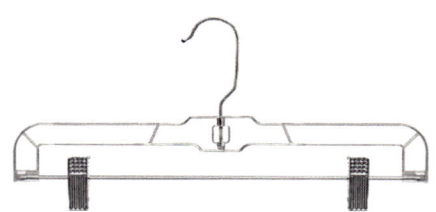

This type for pants and skirts.

Sort by Type: Once your hangers have arrived, and your editing is finished, it's time to reassemble your closet in a thoughtful way.

First, you're going to sort your clothes by type. This can be whatever categories you choose and whatever makes it easiest for you. The key is to be able to find things quickly, easily, not labor over it, not wonder where it is, and not waste time searching for it.

If you sort by type then you can say, "I need a cami today, and I know exactly where to go." For example, I sort by sleeveless, short-sleeved, and long-sleeved tops. You don't have to break it down that much, but I tend to look specifically for sleeve length. Other categories I use for my closet are: jackets, blazers, shorts, skirts, and pants. I put jeans in my drawers. I also put tees and activewear in my drawers.

Determine categories based on your closet space, preferences, and lifestyle. If you don't have enough space in your closet for everything, remember off-season should be elsewhere, and you can also store specialty pieces in other closets or under your bed.

ERIN BUSBEE | STYLE MADE SIMPLE

Sort by Color: You might say to yourself, "I really need a black, short-sleeved blouse." You can immediately go to your section with the short-sleeved tops and pull out a black option. It's very quick and easy.

Whether you go dark-to-light, like the KonMari method, or light-to-dark, or some other color system, is totally up to you. Just come up with a system that works best for you. If a certain item is printed and patterned, and you don't know where to put it, add it to the section where the colors are the most similar. For example, if it's a mostly brown animal print blouse, add it to your brown section. Don't sweat the little details. Find a system that works for you and one that you will remember. There is NO right or wrong here.

Handbags: With handbags, I create shelf dividers and put the bags in a slot on the shelf. There are also handbag shapers if you're worried about keeping the shape of your handbags. You can use these shapers, or you can use tissue paper, which is a lot cheaper and easier for retaining bag shape. You can put dust covers or clear covers over the more expensive bags or use bins for your handbags. The Container Store sells some beautiful linen handbag bins so you can still see the bags peeping out the top.

Boots and Shoes: For tall boots, put pool noodles or boot trees in your boots (available at Amazon or The Container Store) to help your boots keep their shape. They're pretty inexpensive. I also like shoe bins. There are clear bins, or the more expensive luxe linen bins. I sort my shoes and boot.

Drawers: Consider having a sock drawer, an underwear drawer, a bra drawer, a t-shirt drawer, a jeans drawer, and whatever else you need. You may still want to color code the drawers. I color code jeans and sort

by cropped, flared, skinny, etc.

For the underwear and socks drawers, you can use dividers. They're really affordable and a game changer. Having the dividers keeps them sorted however you want, such as color, type, etc.

Jewelry: Having your jewelry on display will help you know that it's there. If you tuck it away, and it's hidden, then it's harder to know that you have it. You forget about it. I used to put all of my jewelry on display in my closet. But in Telluride, Colorado, the housing prices are much higher. One of the sacrifices I made was closet space. Now, I put all my jewelry in my nightstand and I use expandable trays to organize by type and color.

If you have room to hang necklaces on necklace stands, they help keep them from getting tangled, and you can see them very clearly. I lay mine neatly in my expandable organizer in the longest section.

Scarves and Belts: Additionally, there are really cool hanging scarf and belt organizers. You can hang them up right alongside your trousers or find the ones that screw into the wall, depending on your closet space.by cropped, flared, skinny, etc.

For the underwear and socks drawers, you can use dividers. They're really affordable and a game changer. Having the dividers keeps them sorted however you want, such as color, type, etc.

While it may not seem like it, closet organization is a vital part of your overall style and your overall sanity! When your closet is nice, esthetically pleasing, and organized, it saves you time, money, and the stress of not being able to find things. It's a game changer that's worth investing time and money in so you have a closet that is like your very own boutique. You will LOVE shopping your own closet once it is edited and organized!

What will you do with all of the clothes you are purging? Donate? Sell? Detail your plan here.

_____
_____
_____
_____

04
Shopping
PART 4

shopping
LIKE A PRO

Can you believe we're at the last section of the workbook? You're so close to the finish line! Now that we've reviewed your body shape, style, basics, and closet, it's almost time for you to hit the stores and get shopping. But I want you to tackle shopping like a pro, so let's talk strategy.

When you have a strategy, it can be a huge time and money saver. You're also going to find better pieces that you're more excited about wearing. I'm going to give you all the resources you need to be a better, smarter, savvier shopper.

Make a List

This is something we do all the time in our daily lives. The same should be true for your clothes shopping. A list helps you know your highest priority. It also keeps you focused, because it can be overwhelming to walk into a store and try to figure out what to buy. A very focused list will help streamline the process. It may also dictate where you shop.

Make sure your list starts with the basics that we covered previously. You need the basics to wear with all those fun, colorful pieces. Get your wardrobe basics checklist; make your very focused list; then go shopping!

Have a Budget

I have worked with clients who told me they needed a new work wardrobe for under $1,000, and they have nothing in their current closet to support the new needs. For only $1,000 it's possible, but more challenging.

Budgets are dependent on how much you need, what your lifestyle is, where you work, etc. Setting a budget for yourself is helpful so you don't wind up getting into debt over your shopping list. Keep in mind when you are crunching your numbers that they are certain pieces you should spend more money on.

Investment Pieces

If you plan to wear certain pieces regularly for years to come, I recommend investing in higher quality items. I would consider the following categories investment-worthy: **Outwear, coats and jackets. The bonus category is jeans.** Remember cost per wear. You might be looking at a handbag that is $500 and think that's crazy expensive, but if you carry it three times per week for even one year, your cost per wear is just under $3.00! If you have a luxury designer bag that costs $2,000 for ten years and only wear it once a month, your cost per wear is less than $2.00, You get the idea.

Do NOT spend a lot on trendier pieces that you don't think you'll wear for that long. I also wouldn't invest a lot of money in special occasion pieces as you are likely to wear it only a few times. If you want to wear something really show-stopping, look at renting from sites like Rent the Runway.

ERIN BUSBEE | STYLE MADE SIMPLE

In-store Shopping

The first thing to think about when you're shopping in a store is where you can get the best deals. I'd recommend the following places for bargains: **Outlet stores (or malls), Nordstrom Rack, Saks Off 5th, Last Call Neiman Marcus, T.J. Maxx and Marshall's.**

When you're searching for your wardrobe basics or investment pieces, you'll want higher quality clothing. You can get higher quality pieces for less when you go to an outlet store or outlet mall.

Thrift Stores

You can definitely find treasures in consignment or thrift stores. Don't be afraid to look online. There are so many online luxury consignment websites now. If you're thinking about a big-ticket item purchase, like a designer bag, for example, check those sites first. My favorite online luxury consignment websites are: **The Real Real, Vestiaire Collective and eBay (be sure to utilize their new authentication program.)**

Flash Sale Websites

A flash sale website offers specific brand sales for very finite amounts of time, usually about three days. These are an amazing resource because of the great deals on designer goods. The only downside is that they don't house the merchandise. That means the shipping often takes longer (unless you pay for expedited shipping, which I usually do). I have made SO many major purchases through flash sale websites, even home goods like rugs. I'm a huge fan. My top three favorites are: **Ruelala.com, Gilt.com, NordstromRack.com.**

> **Promo codes are another great resource with online shopping.**

Online Shopping

If you are a big online shopper (like me), and you know that's where you're going to do the bulk of your shopping, sign up for individual store sale alert emails. If you're worried about the influx of emails, you can set up a separate email account just for sales. Promo codes are another great resource with online shopping. There are websites dedicated to finding existing, working, active promo codes, like **Retail Me Not and Honey,** which has an extension that you can add to your browser. The extension will tell you if there's an active promo code via a message saying, "Hey, don't forget to click on me to see if you can save extra money." It's free and very easy to use.

What are three websites you can sign up for right now to get discount codes?

_____

_____

_____

Renting Clothing

If you've got a black-tie event, a gala, a charity event, or somebody's wedding and you don't want to invest in a specialty dress, go to a site like Rent the Runway. You can rent a gown, the jewelry to go with it, and the bag to go with it. Rental services you can try: **Rent the Runway (clothing), Bag, Borrow, or Steal (handbags), Switch (jewelry).**

ERIN BUSBEE | STYLE MADE SIMPLE

These tips will help you save time and money, and help you stay focused on getting those high-quality basics that you need, while staying on budget. They're going to help you shop like a confident, self-assured pro, no question!

Don't forget all of your styling tips when wearing your new clothes. Keep those in the back of your mind, including your signature style, which should serve as your go-to outfit combination on days when you are not sure what to wear or need to dress to impress. Great style is what sets you apart and makes you stand out.

> **Shop like a confident, self-assured pro, no question!**

now YOU'RE READY

Congratulations! You did it! You took your measurements and got real about your body shape. You understand your body much better now and how to dress so you create more visual proportion.

You focused on your style type and those three words that encapsulate your essence. You've got your basics covered. You cleaned out and organized your closet, and you are ready to shop and style like a pro!

Keep reminding yourself: *when you look good, you feel good.* This isn't some frivolous thing. It's an integral part of self-care. You might get side-tracked or lost with your style because you are so busy taking care of everyone else, but please come back to this journey. When you do, you will become a more confident, empowered woman who has more to give everyone else in your life. You will be a better wife, mother, sister, friend, and neighbor.

If you feel like you want or need more help elevating your personal style, don't forget to check out our style blogs through the website, *BusbeeStyle.com* and our video tutorials on our YouTube channel. There's NO reason to go through your style journey alone.

YOU CAN DO THIS. I BELIEVE IN YOU.

You deserve to take care of you.

ERIN BUSBEE | STYLE MADE SIMPLE

fashion DICTIONARY

Sharing some common fashion terms to help you be a more informed shopper.

Blazer	A blazer is a jacket with long sleeves and lapels with either gold or silver buttons. It can be worn alone both casually or more formally.
Batwing/Dolman Sleeve	Sleeves that are very full under the arm. They are almost cape-like, resembling the wings of a bat.
Bishop Sleeve	Sleeves that widen gradually to the wrist and then are gathered into a tightly fitting cuff.
Brocade	A rich, ornate fabric with elaborate designs like flowers, foliage, and scrollwork.
Empire Waist	When the waistline is just under the bust.
Epaulettes	A strip of fabric on the shoulders that is inspired by military uniforms.
Fit and Flair	A dress that is form-fitting through the body with a skirt that flairs out at the waist toward the hemline.
Inseam	The seam in a pair of pants sometimes referred to as leg length. You can measure inseam by measuring from the crotch, down to the hemline of your pants.
Jacket	An outer garment with a hemline either to the waist or the hips, typically having sleeves, and fastening some way in the front.
Paper Bag Pants	Pants with extra fabric at the waist that you belt or tie.
Peplum	A ruffle that extends below the waistline of a jacket or blouse.
Ruching	Gathered fabric on an area of the garment made by pleating fabric.
Tapered Leg	Pant legs that become more narrow toward the ankle, usually with a relaxed fit.
Tweed	A coarse wool fabric often woven with different color threads.

frequently ASKED QUESTIONS

Can I wear unique color combinations together like navy and black, and black and brown?
Yes! These colors look wonderful together. I like to have an anchor piece to tie them together. For example, with brown and black, you can wear a pair of leopard print heels that have both black and brown.

Sheer nylons... yay or nay?
I have yet to find the perfect pair that I feel confident and comfortable wearing, but if you have cracked the code and found the perfect pair, by all means! Kate Middleton looks fab in hers!

Can I wear denim on denim?
Another fervent yes. You can try mixing denim tones if you feel strange about wearing two similar colors together. You can even try white or black jeans with a blue denim jacket.

If I am between sizes, what size should I order?
I would order both sizes, and send one back. If you don't want to go that route, double check the size chart again and see which measurements most closely match your own. When in doubt, go big.

Can I wash delicates at home without going to the dry cleaner?
I don't take anything to the dry cleaner. They always come back looking worn. Wash your delicates in a garment bag, in the gentle cycle with cold water and gentle detergent. DO NOT use the dryer. Hang or lay flat to dry. I do this with sweaters, silks, etc.

How do you dress up with small kids?
I have always dressed up regardless of what I'm doing, I just make sure I'm wearing functional shoes. If I get something on my jacket, top, pants, etc., everything can be washed. And, if it gets ruined, it gets ruined. If I worry about that, I'll never wear my clothes!

I have broad shoulders. Can I wear shoulder pads?
In general, if you are broad-shouldered, you'll want to avoid shoulder building details like shoulder pads, puff shoulders, and portrait necklines.

What pieces should I spend more money on?
Don't invest in trendy pieces, spend more on those pieces you will wear for years to come like handbags, jackets, blazers, and jeans. Make sure they are versatile and classic.

Notes

Notes

Made in the USA
Monee, IL
13 October 2021